AF574780

TO THE OFFICE AND BACK

More people in cartoons

Also by Graham

OH SIDNEY — NOT THE WALNUT TREE

> 'Sure the next train has gone ten minutes ago.'
>
> PUNCH. *Vol. 60, page 206. 1871.*

'Season!'

TO THE OFFICE AND BACK

MORE PEOPLE IN CARTOONS

GEOFFREY BLES 1967

SBN: 7138 0188 3

Printed in Great Britain
by Cox & Wyman Ltd, Fakenham

Published by
Geoffrey Bles Ltd
52 Doughty Street, London, W.C.1

First published 1967

'You pays your money and you takes your choice.'

PUNCH. *Vol. 10, p. 17. 1846.*

Contents

INTRODUCTION

It was suggested by a friend (my wife actually) that it might be a good idea to introduce the various sections of this collection of drawings from *Punch* by apt quotations from earlier (*much* earlier) editions of that magazine. The research involved gave me a fascinating hour or two in the library at 10 Bouverie Street; and it was surprising to discover how easy it was to find appropriate phrases from *Punch* of the 19th century to tie in with cartoons of the 1960s.

This does not mean, I hasten to add, that the same old jokes are still coming up; but certainly a number of the subjects from which today's cartoonists draw their material were being well covered by our distinguished predecessors of seventy and more years ago. Including, surprisingly enough, commuting to the office and back.

To the Office and Back is, in fact the title of this collection. There is no particular reason for this choice (though it does fit nicely on the cover) except that those commuting drawings were put on the opening pages by the lay-out expert. (My wife actually.) It is, in fact, the one subject covered of which I personally know little or nothing.

Living in the country as I do, when I go to London I make a point of catching no up train earlier than the 10.18, and am prepared to risk a seizure by sprinting along the Strand to ensure getting, at the latest, the 4.20 down. And not only to avoid the excess on my day ticket either! My information is, that in the battle to board these peak-hour trains, delicate typists are often trampled underfoot and left for dead; elderly clerks may be rammed between train and platform, and seven or eight people standing in the lavatory is not unusual. If *that's* the sort of thing that goes on, the seasoned regulars can have any train between the 4.20 and the 6.30 all to themselves.

Apart from commuting, there are other subjects covered in this book. I am on more familiar ground with most of them (though not yet qualified for the Old Folk's Outing on page 48) since quite a few of those things did actually happen to me. Perhaps they happened to you too?

NOTE

These drawings originally appeared in Punch *and are reproduced by permission of the magazine.*

TO THE OFFICE AND BACK

'Mama! Why do all the tunnels smell so strong of brandy.'

PUNCH. *Vol. 49, p. 156. 1865.*

'There they go, poor devils.'

'Season!'

'You'd have thought they could've put on another carriage.'

'Cut it a bit fine this morning, didn't he?'

'Oho! . . . travelling second on a first ticket, is it?'

'Could be an anagram, I suppose.'

'Is that tiny little space taken?'

'They've all gone sleepy-byes.'

'This is why I usually try to avoid business trains.'

'You know damn well it's my turn to sit next to Miss Ellsworthy.'

'Now you won't forget to waken me at Tonbridge, will you, old man?'

'What worries me is those spare ribs of pork in the oven.'

'Not mine, old man . . . I thought he was yours.'

'Well fancy that! . . . and it's been a lovely day here.'

'Good heavens! . . . That time already?'

MONEY

> 'Nothink for nothink 'ere, and precious little for sixpence.'
>
> PUNCH. *Vol. 57, p. 152. 1869.*

'I'm working on yours at the moment.'

I Know a Bank

'Aw come on, Dad . . .'

'Thought I'd just pop in and check up on the old overdraft.'

'What put you on to collecting threepennies?'

'I wonder if you found a pigskin glove in the night safe this morning?'

'Security, Mr. Bain, security – all I want is a little security.'

'He ate my cheque book again.'

'Back dated to the first of April?'

'There I was . . . prosperous little business . . . nice house . . . car . . . money in the bank . . . Then I won £75,000 on the pools . . .'

'Come along now, sir! . . . we're closing!'

AN ANNOUNCEMENT TO MAKE

''Aving said all I am going to say on this point, I will return to what I was just coming to when I was interrupted, and repeat what I was prevented from saying.'

PUNCH. *Vol. 123, p. 105. 1902.*

'Finally Mrs. Faraday tells me there are still a few hand-knitted oven gloves available at the W.I. stall.

'For the second successive year the classics prize goes to . . .'

'We are interrupting Professor Pirbright's talk for a gale warning.'

'I am happy to say that good progress is being made with the restoration work.'

'. . . your partners for the supper waltz.'

'Entry number 34 is therefore disqualified.'

'It is with regret that I have once again to announce an increase in fees.'

ON WHEELS

> '. . . it's the 'ammer, 'ammer, 'ammer along the 'ard 'igh road.'
>
> PUNCH. *Vol. 30, p. 218. 1856.*

'Let's start off by giving the whole thing a jolly good dust.'

'Sid's had a terrible morning – he had to pass two in succession!'

'Then she says "Well, have I passed?"'

Taxi!

'Haw! I want to go to Hammersmith.'

'Just come from there, Sir. Going t'other way now.'

'Wa'al. You can turn round, can't you?'

PUNCH.
Circa 1900.

*'I **am** sorry . . . I was waving to Mrs. Meredith.'*

'May we smoke?'

'Just take us to the sort of club we don't 'ave back 'ome in Bootle.'

'You're worrying about how much to tip, aren't you?'

'I'd tell you what I think of you, mate, if I didn't 'ave a Bishop in 'ere!'

'The fare's seven-and-threepence, so that's three-and-sevenpence-halfpenny each, but you paid for the coffees, didn't you? So if you give me two-and-sixpence and I give you threepence, because remember I tipped the waitress, then that should be . . .'

'He's silly about cars.'

'Lovely six-and-a-half-pound boy just as I was drawing into the forecourt.'

HEALTH

'What sort of a doctor is he?'
'Oh well, I don't know very much about his ability; but he's got a very good bedside manner.'

PUNCH. *Vol. 86, p. 121. 1884.*

'Aha! a little tenderness there.'

'Some of us have been hanging around here since quarter-to-nine, you know.'

'I take it you're fully qualified, sonny?'

'It's the old back-ache again, Doc.'

*'**Tomorrow**, I said! . . . you can get up tomorrow!'*

'Don't I even get a bottle then?'

'He was telling me about his insomnia, when he suddenly dropped off.'

'Incidentally this stuff's also excellent for removing fruit stains from table linen.'

'Everything?'

'I'll tell you what he's doing! – he's sitting at his desk reading his newspaper, that's what he's doing!'

A Touch of Insomnia

'Is life worth living?' . . . he suspects it is, in a great measure, a question of the Liver.
PUNCH. *Vol. 73, p. 207. 1877.*

'There's a box of blue pills here . . . shall I try one of them?'

'Tom? It's me! I've just had a thought about the Phillipson contract.'

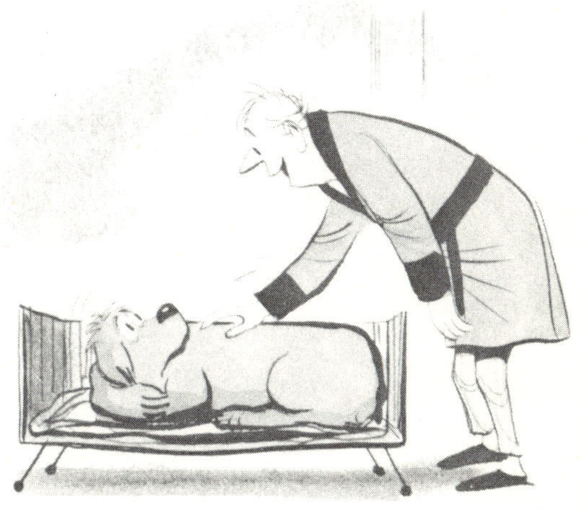

'Walkies?'

'Just tidying up the rose-border.'

'Do you want mustard in yours?'

'What time does Jack de Manio come on?'

'How on earth did you get your sheet into that state?'

'Coffee?'

'. . . generous and unexpected gift . . . believe me, could tell a few stories . . . can remember when Master Henry was an apprentice . . . seen many changes in dear old firm . . . if I may, word of advice to younger members of staff . . . happiest years of my life . . . no electronic computers in those days . . . make way for younger man . . .'

'. . . er . . . not much of a hand at speechifying . . . luckiest man in the world . . . er . . . my wife and I . . . awfully nice things said by previous speaker . . . hope to see you all at 24 Acacia Road . . . not all at once, ha, ha . . . Mr. Earnshaw – or should I say Dad . . . er . . . charming bridesmaids . . . er . . . behalf of us both . . .'

SPEECH DAY

Here was an old owl liv'd in
an oak
The more he heard, the less
he spoke;
The less he spoke, the more
he heard
O, if men were all like that
wise bird.

PUNCH. *Vol. 68, p. 155. 1875.*

'. . . speechless . . . those beautiful, beautiful flowers . . . wonderful, wonderful audience . . . inspiration to any artist . . . this lovely, lovely theatre . . . always a joy to come to your beautiful city . . . heartwarming reception . . . behalf of us all . . . thank you, thank you . . . bottom of my heart . . .'

'Turning out on such a miserable night . . . remarkable versatility shown by choir members . . . not forgetting workers behind scenes . . . Mr. Gibson who rose from sickbed to help with electrical wiring . . . these days of TV and canned entertainment . . . homespun talent . . . healthy fillip for organ fund . . . silver collection now be taken . . .'

'Spirit of the desert still survives . . . finest body of men ever had honour to command . . . ordinary British chap . . . proved himself in battle . . . if may reminisce . . . that fateful night . . . decision wholly mine . . . caught the old fox napping . . . had our tails up . . . took part in making of history . . . kicked him out of Africa . . .'

'Pleasant duty has fallen on me . . . distinguished old girl . . . kind of her to give up valuable time . . . words of wisdom . . . stand us in good stead in later life . . . not forgetting amusing humorous anecdotes . . . modest about her own scholastic abilities . . . always honoured to see her at college . . . call on you all to give . . . hip, hip . . .'

REVEREND GENTLEMEN

'Ah whiles ha'e ma doobts aboot the meenister.'

PUNCH. *Vol. 79, p. 275. 1880.*

'It won't make them drowsy, will it?'

'Still no ideas yet, dear?'

'Oh, my goodness – the Renshaw wedding!'

'I just don't seem to send them as I used to.'

'Sorry to be a nuisance.'

'Shouldn't you be out visiting the sick or something?'

'Frankly it'll be a ruddy miracle if we're finished by July.'

'Actually he's playing in a golf ma—'

'Gallivanting about on that thing!'

'How much do you reckon we'll take?'

'Why not try . . . you know . . . just a few simple words.'

OLD PEOPLE

Tourist (to Oldest Inhabitant): 'And what is the population of this village?'
Oldest Inhabitant. 'Well, Zur, there's me – and – ' (*long pause*) 'Well, Zur, I don't exactly know 'ow many more they be.'

PUNCH. *Vol. 124, p. 17. 1903.*

'You sat next to the vicar on the choir outing.'

'Remember last year – that mods and rockers battle?'

'Twist.'

'Doesn't Mr. Henderson look **nice** *in his braces?'*

'It's really lovely once you're in.'

'Of course, it hasn't got the comfort of my son-in-law's Cortina.'

'We're all down here on the beach, Mr. Delaney.'

'He's never . . .!'

'We shouldn't have stopped at that pub.'

YOUNG PEOPLE

'Never do today what you can put off till tomorrow.'

PUNCH. *Vol. 17, p. 241. 1849.*

'We have a fine relationship, you and I, Bill . . . more like pals than father and son, with give and take on both sides – so for God's sake will you go out and get yourself a haircut.'

'Anyway to get back to this rat we were dissecting . . .'

'Surely it's long past his bedtime.'

Younger People

> 'Go directly – see what she's doing, and tell her she mustn't.'
>
> PUNCH. *Vol. 68, p. 202. 1872.*

'Daddy! Mickey's got a Geography test first period!'

'The kiss of life – to a goldfish?'

'Mummy!! Quick!!'

'We have a suspicion there may be a wolf under Timmy's bed.'

'It's a man from the N.S.P.C.C.!'

'Damming the stream to make a paddling pool . . .!'

FRIENDS

'Advice to persons about to marry. – Don't.'

PUNCH. *Vol. 8, p. 1. 1845.*

'As I see it, Sid, you've lost a daughter and gained a nit.'

A Friend for the Week-End

Guest (to Host who hates getting up early). 'I'm so awfully sorry to have dragged you up at this unearthly hour, but I had to catch the 8.30 train.'
Host. 'Not at all. I'm only too glad to see you off!'

PUNCH. *Circa 1900.*

'Just wondering where you keep the gin, old man . . .'

'NOBODY needs two baths a day . . .!'

'If only I could explain to you about Harry not liking dogs . . .'

'What say we all stroll down to the local before lunch . . .?'

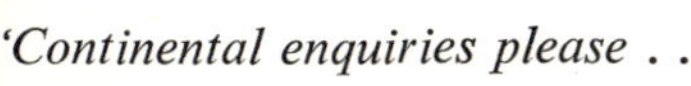

'Continental enquiries please . . .'

'It's all right . . . he was only gargling . . .'

'Probably for me . . .'

'Great news! . . . They don't need me at the office on Monday . . .'

THE WEATHER

> 'Most 'strordinary weather, ain't it? First it's 'ot, then it's cold. Blow me if one knows how to dress.'
>
> PUNCH. *Vol. 117, p. 255. 1899.*

'Coach leaves at six-thirty, doesn't it?'

*'If mist there be o'er Gurlford Peak,
'Tis plastic macs for rest of week.'*

'Not bad, really . . . sunny, but always a cold wind with it . . .'

RECORD
TEMPERATURE
ON
AIR MINISTRY
ROOF

GALES
SWEEP
COAST